The SOUTHERN in Surrey & Berkshire

Frontispiece: 'West Country' class, No. 34107, *Blandford Forum* on the 5.00 pm Waterloo to Salisbury train in Goldsworth Cutting between Woking and Brookwood on 16th May 1964.

The SOUTHERN in Surrey & Berkshire

Terry Gough

Oxford Publishing Co.

ISBN 0 86093 426 8

A FOULIS-OPC Railway Book

Published by:
Haynes Publishing Group
Sparkford, Near Yeovil, Somerset. BA22 7JJ

Haynes Publications Inc.
861 Lawrence Drive, Newbury Park, California 91320, USA

British Library Cataloguing in Publication Data
Gough, Terry
    The Southern in Surrey and Berkshire.
    1. Surrey. Railway services : British Rail.
    Southern Region. Steam locomotives, 1951–
    1961 – Illustrations 2. Berkshire. Railway
    services. British Rail. Southern Region.
    Steam locomotives, 1957–1967
    I. Title
    625.2'61'094221

    ISBN 0-86093-426-8

Abbreviations

BR .... British Railways
GWR .... Great Western Railway
LBSCR .... London, Brighton & South Coast Railway
LMSR .... London, Midland & Scottish Railway
LNER .... London & North Eastern Railway
LSWR .... London & South Western Railway
SECR .... South Eastern & Chatham Railway
SER .... South Eastern Railway
SR .... Southern Railway

BC .... brake composite
BCK .... brake composite corridor
BT .... brake third
BTK .... brake third corridor
C .... composite
CK .... composite corridor
FK .... first corridor
T .... third
TK .... third corridor
TO .... third open

Contents

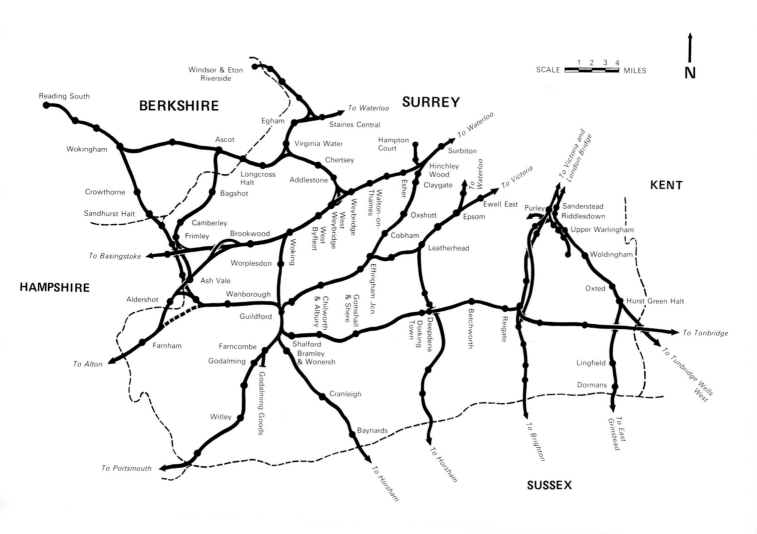

INTRODUCTION

Most present day users of the extensive outer suburban network of the Southern Region are probably not aware that the railways of Surrey go back to the very beginning of railway development. The first public railway in the world, which used open horse drawn wagons, was built in Surrey with the intention of linking London and Portsmouth through the Merstham Gap. The first steam operated railway was opened in 1838 by the London & Southampton Railway Company from Nine Elms to Woking Common, thus marking the beginning of the present day main line from London to the South West. When the line was opened, there was no urban development and Surbiton as such did not exist, the main line station at this point being called Kingston. The situation was the same at Woking, where the town was about two miles from the railway station. Within a year the line was extended to Basingstoke and in 1845 Woking became a junction when the line to Guildford was built.

It was not long before lines to other parts of Surrey were constructed, from Weybridge to Chertsey in 1848 – even before the Portsmouth main line had reached Godalming. By 1856 the London & South Western Railway had lines through Staines to Virginia Water and to Wokingham in Berkshire, where it joined the South Eastern Railway near the end of its line from Redhill. In the succeeding years lines were built to Farnham and Alton, Frimley and Bagshot and a new line between Surbiton and Guildford, via Oxshott and Cobham. Guildford also had a line to Horsham, which was opened in 1865 by the London, Brighton & South Coast Railway and there were thus lines radiating in six directions from here.

The London, Brighton & South Coast Railway had its own main line from London to Portsmouth. Although built piecemeal, it eventually connected Epsom, Leatherhead, Dorking and Horsham and was known as the Mid Sussex Line. However, its value as a route to Portsmouth was severely affected once the London & South Western Railway was able to use the more direct route through Woking and Guildford. More importantly, the LBSCR had a direct link between London and Brighton, built in 1841. A railway was also built between Croydon and East Grinstead and was operated jointly for most of its length by the London, Brighton & South Coast and the South Eastern Railway companies. This formed a vital connection between London and a number of secondary lines which served rural Sussex and eventually reached the South Coast.

By the turn of the century, the railway system in Surrey and Berkshire was virtually complete. Subsequent growth of towns served by the railway has been phenomenal. Some places anticipated the arrival of the railway which never materialised. One such example is Chobham, which even to this day has a Station Road, although there has never been a railway, let alone a station at Chobham. The railway companies increased their services to meet the demands of the public, who began to realise that the railway offered them the facility for living in the countryside, but with ready access to London. The commuting age was thus born. This is well illustrated by Woking. A new town has grown up round the railway, which forms the commercial and residential centre of present day Woking. Old Woking, for which the railway was built, is by contrast still very much a village. Woking is not a railway town in the same sense as, for example, Eastleigh further down the line, because it does not rely on the railway as a primary employer. It does, however, rely very heavily on the railway to transport thousands of people to London for employment every working day of the year. Present day Woking is extremely busy and trains from London are divided here for stations further south and west. There is even a rail-air coach link to Heathrow Airport for the benefit of rail travellers. The only regret is that there is no longer a direct service to Reading, which has to be reached via Guildford or Basingstoke. Unfortunately freight, as in the rest of the county, is now only a trickle and the large yards at Woking are used for engineers' trains. The town of Surbiton also established itself round the railway and is now one of the major commuting centres of South East England.

The basic network remained almost unaltered up to and including the Southern Railway period. Even after Nationalization, very little was cut back and the vast majority of lines and stations are in regular use today. The only major losses have been the Guildford to Horsham branch in 1965 and the effect which massive closures in Sussex have had on the Oxted line. There have, however, been dramatic changes in the type and pattern of services, resulting from electrification, initiated in the London area prior to Grouping of the railway companies, but extended into Surrey and beyond with great enthusiasm by the Southern Railway. The extremity of the London & South Western Railway's electrified lines was Claygate and this was extended to Guildford in 1926. The main line to Brighton was electrified in Surrey as far as Redhill in 1932. Most of the former London & South Western lines were electrified in 1937, including the main line from Surbiton to Woking and thence the Portsmouth and Alton lines. Lines in North Surrey and Berkshire were electrified two years later, but further plans were interrupted by the war. The electric stock for the suburban and secondary routes was in many cases rebuilt from pre-Grouping steam hauled coaches, but main line trains were new. Each main line had characteristic stock, the Portsmouth trains having corridor connections between each set, in contrast to the Brighton main line, whose stock did not have inter-set connections. Sets for semi-fast trains on the main lines were also composed of corridor coaches, but without gangways between individual coaches. These sets survived until the British Railways' electrification programme was under way, which included electrification beyond the Woking area to Basingstoke and Bournemouth.

Every time electrification spread, more steam engines were inevitably made redundant. On the London to Brighton line, which has become one of the busiest lines in the country, steam was very rarely seen. On the former London & South Western lines, only the main line services through Woking were steam operated, the other lines only seeing steam on special workings and freight trains, even prior to World War II. On the former South Eastern Railway, the Redhill to Reading line remained steam operated until the advent of diesel power in the 1960s. Although part of the line was subsequently included in the electrification plans of 1969, it is still diesel worked. This was a superb line to see both passenger and freight trains hard at work. One major change which took place on this line 20 years ago was the complete destruction of the facilities at Reading and the deviation of all Southern Region trains to the Western Region main line station. The Oxted line was not electrified until 1987, although there were such plans before Nationalization and periodically thereafter. The line offered excellent opportunities for steam hauled travel and photography, with its regular service from London and fairly harshly graded terrain. But eventually it was given over to diesel operation,

Class 700, No. 30697 being attached to two pre-Grouping coaches at Cranleigh, to form the 1.09 pm Saturdays only train to Guildford on 2nd April 1960.

Leaving the 'down' bay at Oxted on 14th April 1960 is Class H No. 31193 and set No. 660 on an all stations train to Tunbridge Wells West.

leaving only the expresses from Waterloo on the Western Section as a stronghold of steam operation, which held out until June 1967.

Now the sight of a steam train in Surrey is just a memory and even the Southern Railway electric sets which hastened the demise of the steam engine have also gone. For that reason, I have included in this volume, which is mostly about the steam engine, just a few photographs of electric trains.

In the early days of the railway, the northern boundary of Surrey extended to central London, but over the decades the boundary has been moved as London has expanded. In compiling this volume, I have taken the post war boundary prior to the formation of the Greater London Council, using as a starting point the most important station at the London end of each line.

Terry Gough, Woking, 1988

Author's Note

The Bournemouth and Weymouth line beyond Woking is covered in the author's book *The Southern in Hampshire and Dorset*, and the West of England lines in *The Southern West of Salisbury*. The lines south of Oxted are included in *The Southern in Kent and Sussex*. Further coverage of the Horsham to Guildford line is given in *Around the Branch Lines, Volume 1* and the Reading to Redhill line in *Cross Country Routes of the Southern*.

Acknowledgement

The author wishes to thank British Railways (Southern Region) for the provision of a lineside permit, enabling him to reach many of the locations shown in this and earlier albums in the series.

Plate 1: Excellent views of the railway were afforded from the two road overbridges at the London end of Surbiton Station. 'King Arthur' class No. 30795 *Sir Dinadan* passes between the bridges on the 7.30 am train from Basingstoke to Waterloo on 28th June 1961. This train, which ran only on Mondays to Fridays, stopped at all stations to Woking, except Brookwood, and then ran non-stop to Waterloo. It was one of several early morning trains from Basingstoke run mainly for the benefit of commuters and was, as a result, always heavily loaded.

Plate 2: Approaching Surbiton on the wrong line as a result of track relaying, is a 'down' Bournemouth train hauled by 'West Country' class No. 34094 *Mortehoe,* one Sunday morning in January 1962. One of the difficulties experienced by the Southern Region was that intensive use of track in the suburban area precluded the carrying out of engineering works during the weekday. As a result, services were frequently disrupted at weekends, resulting in wrong line working, diversions, or alternative bus services. All of this was rather frustrating for the passenger, but often produced interesting workings, such as shown here.

Plate 3: The best Bournemouth trains were often worked by 'Merchant Navy' class Pacifics, which ran non-stop, at least to Basingstoke. Every morning there was, however, a lesser train, which called at Surbiton, officially at least, only to pick up passengers. Those in the know could use this train between Waterloo and Surbiton, as a welcome change from travelling by electric train. On 8th July 1956, the train was worked by 'Merchant Navy' class No. 35016 *Elders Fyffes,* and is crossing from the 'down' through line to the local line at the east end of Surbiton Station. The line on the far right is for Hampton Court trains. A London Transport trolleybus is crossing the road bridge, on route 601 which ran from Tolworth to Twickenham. The motive power on both the road and railway has now passed into history.

Plate 4: Plenty of steam power at Surbiton on this occasion in February 1962, with two engineers' trains on the 'down' lines. The Mogul is No. 31813, ready to leave on an empty ballast train to Wilton South. A passenger train heading for the West of England is using the 'up' through line and is hauled by 'Merchant Navy' class No. 35017 *Belgian Marine.* Surbiton was a modern style SR station, built just prior to World War II to replace the original station, which was known successively as Kingston, Kingston Junction and Surbiton & Kingston. The SR built a signal box on the 'up' side of the line at the country end of the station, but this was replaced by a new box on the opposite side of the line in 1970. This controlled the main line between Berrylands and West Byfleet and the lines to Hampton Court, Effingham Junction and Chertsey.

Plate 5: On Saturdays, the pattern of services was rather different and in summer catered predominantly for the holiday traffic to the West. This photograph of an evening train from Basingstoke, taken at Surbiton on 7th July 1962, shows most unusual motive power in the form of Class T9 No. 120 in LSWR colours. This is not a special train, but the 7.40 pm Basingstoke to Waterloo semi-fast service. This engine was used for several Saturdays on the Basingstoke trains and made a memorable sight, reminiscent of pre-war days when T9s were used on many main line trains. The effect is marred by the use of rolling stock built in 1947.

Plate 6: A freight train on the 'down' local line west of Surbiton, hauled by ex LSWR Class 700 No. 30701, on 28th September 1959. Despite its appearance, the brake van is not one of the numerous standard SR 25 ton vehicles, but is one of a few 15 ton vans (see Plate 33).

Plate 7: A train usually entrusted to a 'King Arthur' class locomotive, even toward the end of steam operations, was the 2.54 pm Waterloo to Basingstoke semi fast service. Passing through Esher Station in the Summer of 1961 is No. 30451 *Sir Lamorak*. The station buildings at Esher are of LSWR origin. These lasted until 1987 when the station was rebuilt and the entrance relocated in the former goods yard approach road.

Plate 8: Several of the intermediate stations between Surbiton and Woking had small yards for coal and other merchandise. At Esher, where this photograph was taken, the yard contained for many years an old SECR birdcage passenger brake van. Shunting here on the morning of 27th July 1955 is Class U No. 31634. All these yards are now closed and most have been converted to car parks for commuters, although at Esher the local coal merchant still operates from the far end of the yard site.

Plate 9: A 'down' "Pompey", approaching Esher on 18th September 1961, the leading unit being 4-RES No. 3062. The term "Pompey" refers to the destination of the train, one of the hourly expresses from Waterloo to Portsmouth Harbour. It was also the nickname given to the electric units, which were built for this service in 1937. They were alternatively referred to as "Nelsons", to reflect their 'one eyed' appearance resulting from the indicator blind on the right hand side of the corridor connection. The Portsmouth expresses usually consisted of three four-car units, one including a restaurant car.

Plate 10: Wrong line working for a breakdown train at Esher on 15th May 1955. The engine is Class 700 No. 30308, the stream crane was built by Ransomes & Rapier and the vehicle on the rear is an ex SECR passenger brake van. The crane had been used over the weekend in relation to bridge replacement at the London end of the station.

Plate 11: An extraordinary sight greeted the photographer at Esher on 16th September 1961, with the 1.12 pm Basingstoke to Waterloo train passing empty carriage stock on the local line being hauled by ex LMSR Class 4F No. 44581 of Cricklewood Depot. The 'up' Basingstoke train is headed by BR Standard Class 5MT No. 73117 *Vivien*.

Plate 12: Esher Station was adjacent to Sandown Park Racecourse and there was direct access to the racecourse from specially built platforms at the country end of the station. On race days these platforms were served by additional electric trains from London. There were two lower quadrant semaphore starters guarding exit from the race platforms, as seen in this photograph taken on 1st September 1955. One was a survivor of an unusual LSWR slotted post design, the arm being retained within the post when not in use, as is the case on this occasion. In the background is Esher Station and an 'up' all stations electric train.

Plate 13:   A 'down' Lymington boat train charging through Walton-on-Thames Station in August 1961. These trains were traditionally worked by the Drummond D15 class, but after their withdrawal, the 'Schools' class engines were often used, in this instance No. 30921 *Shrewsbury*.

Plate 14:   Summer Saturdays caused severe strain on the ability of the railway to provide sufficient rolling stock for the extra trains needed to cope with the holiday traffic. Coaching stock was stored at a number of suburban locations and at various points on the main line, as far away as Basingstoke. Early on Saturday mornings there was a procession of empty stock workings from these locations to Waterloo. One such place was Oatlands Park near Weybridge and this illustration shows Class Q1 No. 33028 on 25th August 1962, setting out for Waterloo with a miscellaneous collection of Maunsell, Bulleid and even an ex LNER coach.

Plate 24: There were two major yards at Woking, one situated on the 'down' side and extending beyond the junction on the Portsmouth line, and the other on the 'up' side parallel with the Bournemouth line. The 'down' yard was for general freight and the 'up' side was the engineers' yard. Both of these yards were active day and night, the engineers' yard being particularly busy at weekends. In this photograph, taken from the west end of Woking Station on 23rd December 1961, a freight train from Eastleigh hauled by Class S15 No. 30496 draws parallel with Class U No. 31628, which is setting back into the engineers' yard. In the background, another SR Mogul is running light.

Plate 25: Class Q1 No. 33012 enters Woking Yard in December 1963 at the end of its short journey from Feltham. There were several freight trains per day between these two points, as Feltham was the main marshalling yard for inter-regional freight transfers and at Woking, stock was sorted for the Portsmouth, Southampton and Exeter lines.

Plate 26: Guildford shed provided a station pilot for Woking, for many years a Class M7 0-4-4 tank engine and after elimination of steam, a class 08 or 09 diesel shunter. Guildford shed also had a Class USA shunter, No. 30064, which turned up at Woking one morning in the Autumn of 1964.

Plate 27: Mid-morning on weekdays was usually a very active time in Woking Yard, with shunting and the arrival of at least one train. In the yard in December 1963 are two ex Southern Railway engines, Class U No. 31617 and Class Q1 No. 33033.

Plate 31: A day spent at Woking was almost certain to produce a variety of motive power, with fre[ight] hauled by SR Moguls, Urie S15s and Q1s and passenger trains hauled by Bulleid Pacifics, 'King Ar[thurs]' 'Lord Nelsons', not to mention a succession of electric trains consisting of SR built 2-BIL and 4-C[OR]. There was still room for surprises, such as this freight train from Feltham, hauled by BR Standard [Class] No. 80012 and a diesel shunting locomotive, entering the 'down' yard on 31st December 1963.

Plate 32: An unidentified BR Standard locomotive approaching the 'up' yard at Woking on a ret[urn] ballast train, one Sunday evening in July 1966. The passenger coach on the rear is a dormitory vehicle, [rebuilt] from Maunsell, Hastings line stock. In the foreground are several sleeper wagons and a rail-carry[ing] wagon.

Plate 37: Another freight train struggling along the 'down' local line between Woking and Brookwood after a heavy snow fall in January 1963. The train is bound for Southampton Docks and is hauled by Class S15 No. 30506.

Plate 38: A few months later the cutting looks rather different as a freight train from Woking and bound ultimately for Ascot trundles along the local line. The engine is SR Class Q No. 30541. These engines were only rarely seen on this part of the Southern Region as most were allocated to Central Section running sheds.

Plate 29: There were no servicing facilities in Woking Yard and engines requiring water would take this from one of the columns situated at the station. Taking water in the bay at the 'down', country end of the station (platform 6) on 14th November 1963 is Class Q1 No. 33009. This bay was used for parcels trains and westbound electric services which occasionally started from Woking. There was another bay at the London end of the same platform, but this was used exclusively for postal traffic. Both bays are still in use.

Plate 30: Because of the proximity of Woking Yard to the main line, it was an easy matter to keep an eye on the expresses passing through Woking. In this view from the yard in the winter of 1963, 'Merchant Navy' class No. 35007 *Aberdeen Commonwealth* is at the head of the 1.00 pm Waterloo to the West of England train.

Plate 39: The first station beyond Woking was Brookwood and, whilst serving only a village, was nevertheless an important station, being the junction for the Bisley Camp and Necropolis branches, and the Alton line. The Bisley branch served the rifle ranges and several army camps. It had no regular passenger service, but ran as the occasion demanded until closure in 1952. Brookwood is still used by large numbers of army personnel who now continue to the camps by road. The Necropolis line, which had a through funeral train service from a special station near Waterloo (and also ran as required!), ceased operations in 1941. Apart from these purely local activities, express trains to Bournemouth and the West passed through Brookwood, often at high speed. One such train was the 1.30 pm Waterloo to Weymouth, which on 9th June 1962 was hauled by 'Merchant Navy' class No. 35021 *New Zealand Line.* On the 'up' local line is 'Lord Nelson' class No. 30857 *Lord Howe,* working the 12.20 pm stopping train from Eastleigh.

Plate 40: Waiting for the right of way at Brookwood on the evening of 25th July 1963 is the 7.40 pm Basingstoke to Waterloo stopping train, hauled by Class 5MT No. 73086 *The Green Knight.*

Plate 45: It was quite a frustrating exercise waiting for the Christmas parcels trains, which rarely ran to anything like their scheduled times. They would frequently come hours late, by which time the photographer had either given up or become so cold that even operating a camera was painful. The other problem over which there was no control was that the weak winter light would fail prior to arrival of the train. A parcels train from Woking to Alton enters Brookwood Station on the afternoon of 23rd December 1961, hauled by Class M7 No. 30378 of Guildford shed.

Plate 46: There was a frequent service of electric trains to Alton. These trains ran from Waterloo and split at Woking, the other portion proceeding to Portsmouth & Southsea. After the Bournemouth line electrification, trains were composed alternately of Alton/Portsmouth and Alton/Basingstoke portions. Although the present day arrangement is that all trains are divided at Woking, for a short while Brookwood became the dividing place for the Alton and Basingstoke trains. The result of serving both Alton and Basingstoke is that, even outside the rush hour periods, Brookwood has a service of four trains per hour in each direction, far higher than the local traffic justifies. On 19th May 1962, electric unit 2-BIL No. 2046 leaves Brookwood for Alton, whilst 'Battle of Britain' class No. 34051 *Winston Churchill* enters the 'up' platform on the 12.58 pm Salisbury to Waterloo service.

Plate 47: 2-BIL electric unit No. 2021 pauses at Ash Vale. This station is situated between Pirbright Junction and Aldershot and is also the junction of the line to Ascot, the latter being single track almost as far as the next station of Frimley. The lines through Ash Vale were included in the pre war electrification scheme and the station was completely rebuilt in 1970. From Ash Vale, Waterloo can be reached either by the direct service through Brookwood or by the Guildford-Aldershot-Ascot service, both of which run at half hourly intervals throughout the day.

Plate 48: A parcels train leaving Woking for the Portsmouth line behind Class M7 No. 30055 on 20th December 1962. This view was taken from the small 'down' yard at the west end of the station, near the goods shed which contains an LSWR style gibbet crane.

WOKING TO WITLEY (PORTSMOUTH LINE)

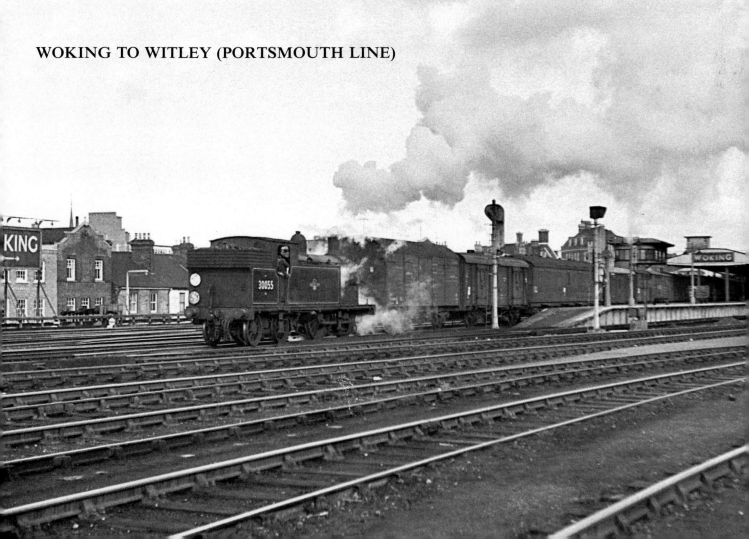

Plate 49: A parcels train from Guildford, consisting of several vans and a passenger coach, passes Woking Yard in the week prior to Christmas 1965. The engine is SR Class N No. 31858 of Guildford shed and was withdrawn from service within days of this photograph being taken, to be cut up a few months later.

Plate 50: A once common sight throughout the British Isles was the cattle train. Movement of livestock had been a long standing commitment of the railways, but early in the 1960s, the decision was made to stop conveying cattle and within a short time, cattle wagons had all but disappeared from the railway scene. In this photograph, taken on the Portsmouth line near Woking on 20th December 1962, an unidentified SR Mogul hauls a freight train, consisting predominantly of cattle wagons, toward London.

Plate 51: A double headed 'down' ballast train from Woking Yard near Worplesdon on 3rd April 1965. The leading engine is Class N No. 31873 and the other engine Class Q1 No. 33006.

Plate 52: A train of empty open wagons hauled by SR Class U No. 31627 crosses Prey Heath near Worplesdon on its way to Guildford on 25th April 1965.

Plate 53: Despite being within the London outer suburban area and having a frequent electric train service, Worplesdon had the air of a country station. The station buildings were virtually unchanged since they were built, apart from minor items such as lighting and nameboards. The only major change was the closing of the yard, demolishing of the signal box and extending the length of the platforms. Worplesdon was the last station in an alliteration of six, beginning at Walton-on-Thames. Unfortunately the series was broken when West Weybridge Station was renamed Byfleet & New Haw in 1961. The centenary of the opening of the station was celebrated in March 1983 with a small display at the station and some local publicity. This is the 'up' platform in 1967.

Plate 54: A 'down' parcels train hauled by Class N No. 31821 on the main line at Guildford Station on 23rd December 1961. Guildford was a major junction and, apart from the Waterloo to Portsmouth service, had trains to and from the Effingham Junction line, Aldershot, Reading, Redhill and Horsham, the last three being steam worked. There was, and indeed still is, a number of inter-regional trains which pass through Guildford, having reached the Southern Region via Reading.

Plate 55: The Portsmouth Direct line was opened from Woking to Guildford in 1845 and by 1849 had reached Godalming, where it had a terminus, which later became Godalming Goods Depot. The line was extended to Havant in 1859, where it joined the existing line to Portsmouth. It was, however, necessary to realign the railway to avoid Crownpits Hill, before building could proceed toward Portsmouth. To mark the centenary of the opening to Havant, a special train was run on 25th January 1959. This ran from Victoria to Surbiton and thence via the Effingham Junction line (referred to as the New Line) to Guildford, Havant and Gosport. It even paid a visit to the site of the original Godalming Station. It returned to London by using the Portsmouth Direct line as far as West Weybridge and thence ran to Virginia Water and Clapham Junction. The centenary special is leaving Guildford in frosty weather behind Class 700 No. 30350 of Guildford shed, which had just been attached for the short run to Godalming Goods Yard.

Plate 56: The main goods yard at Guildford was situated at the London end of the station on the 'down' side. On the 'up' side were sidings for berthing electric units. At the Portsmouth end of the station, there was a tunnel under the North Downs which at this point are dissected by the River Wey and so constitute a relatively easy path for the railway. Between the station and the tunnel on the 'down' side were a couple of sidings occasionally used for vans traffic. Viewed from the running sheds opposite, on 22nd April 1964, is Class 2MT No. 41287, depositing a BR general utility van in the far siding.

Plate 58: Steam hauled passenger trains were very unusual on the Portsmouth line. However, trains occasionally used this route to Bournemouth at weekends when there were major engineering works west of Woking or in the Winchester and Southampton area. Another alternative route to Bournemouth was via the Itchen Valley through Alresford and this was normally used if the main line was occupied between Pirbright Junction and Winchester Junction. A Waterloo to Bournemouth train hauled by 'West Country' class No. 34044 *Woolacombe,* diverted via the Portsmouth Direct line, is seen between Farncombe and Godalming on 12th September 1964. The old main line, which terminated at Godalming, is on the right (see Plate 55).

Plate 59: Several of the Portsmouth line stations were built to a similar style, including the second of the Godalming stations. It is remarkable how little most of these stations have changed, despite the SR electrification programme and various aspects of modernization in BR days. This photograph shows Witley in 1967.

Plate 60: Most of the stations were still gas-lit up to the late 1960s. This photograph at Witley in 1967 shows a standard SR swan neck gas lamp, which had been added to an LSWR post fitted originally with a lantern style oil lamp. The station nameplate is the SR green enamel type with white lettering. These have now been replaced by simple rectangular plates consisting of black lettering on a white background, attached to the metal post of a fluorescent light. Incidentally, Godalming was the first town in England to install electric street lighting, so the railway was many decades behind the times in this sense.

Plate 61: (Previous page)   The running shed consisted of two main buildings, a long house and adjacent round house. The long house was situated parallel to the main line and extended right to the tunnel mouth. The round house, or to be more precise the half-round house, was tucked up against chalk downs. In this photograph, taken on 27th August 1960, both sheds can be seen, with Class 700 No. 30694 entering the shed yard from the main line. Along the outside wall of the long house is the breakdown train. Schools class No. 30906 *Sherborne* simmers by the side of the roundhouse.

Plate 62:   The shed yard extended under the main road overbridge at the end of the station to the coaling stage, which was a corrugated asbestos structure and is visible in the background. Class B4 No. 30089 is acting as shed pilot on 31st May 1962 and shunting some wagons at the coaling plant is Class Q1 No. 33037.

Plate 63: Following withdrawal of the B4 locomotive in the Spring of 1963, a USA class tank engine was allocated to Guildford for pilot duties. On 10th October 1963 this task was being undertaken by No. 30072. This engine was withdrawn in 1967 and was purchased for the Keighley & Worth Valley Railway, where it may now be seen.

Plate 64: The Maunsell Class Z 0-8-0 tank locomotives were intended for heavy shunting duties. There were only eight engines, which were built in 1929 at Brighton Works. They were allocated to depots responsible for supplying motive power for the major SR marshalling yards in Kent, the London area and as far away as Exmouth Junction. With the advent of diesel shunters, they were gradually displaced and eventually all eight finished up in use as bankers for heavy trains between Exeter St David's and Exeter Central stations. The first member of the class, No. 30950, paid a short visit to Guildford during 1960, where it was seen on 27th August shunting a few wagons under the coaling stage. The whole class was withdrawn during the last three months of 1962.

Plate 65: Guildford shed provided some of the motive power for the Reading to Redhill line, which had a frequent passenger and freight service and was worked most commonly by SR 2-6-0 tender engines. Being turned on 31st May 1962 is class U No. 31800, which had just worked a train from Redhill. Four members of the U Class have been preserved, two being on the Mid-Hants Railway and two on the Bluebell Railway.

Plate 66: One type of engine which regrettably was not preserved and was an early casualty once the BR Modernization programme had been announced, was the LSWR Class 0395. These engines, of which there were 70, were built by Neilson and Company of Glasgow between 1881 and 1886 for main line goods work. Disposal began as early as 1916, when many were sent to the Middle East. Only 18 were taken into BR stock and by 1957, when this photograph was taken of No. 30578 at Guildford, there were only six left. These were allocated to Eastleigh, Guildford and Feltham, the last survivor being withdrawn two years later.

Plate 67: The New Line refers to the alternative route between Surbiton and Guildford, which ran south of the main line, via Cobham and Effingham Junction. It was only new in the sense that it succeeded chronologically the original route through Woking and was opened in 1885. It left the main line at the same place as the Hampton Court branch, at Long Ditton, 2½ miles west of Surbiton. Only third class accommodation was provided, usually in the form of a 4-SUB electric unit, until the introduction of BR built electric multiple units when first class accommodation was included. Photographed at Surbiton on 1st February 1961 is 4-SUB No. 4311, bound for Guildford. The headcode is the old SR style stencil, using letters of the alphabet, rather than the system using numerals on roller blinds. The letter 'H' referred to Waterloo to Hampton Court services and 'H bar' to the New Line.

Plate 68: Claygate was the first station on the New Line after Surbiton until the SR built an intermediate station at Hinchley Wood in 1930. There were also stations for the villages of Oxshott and Cobham, before reaching Effingham, where there was a junction for Leatherhead. The line from Leatherhead provided a link between the LSWR and LBSCR. There were small yards at stations on the New Line to deal with local goods traffic. On 3rd April 1965, Class Q1 No. 33018 is engaged in shunting at Cobham. As a reminder of pre-Nationalization days, someone has chalked the original number, C18, on the engine's smokebox door.

Plate 69: The New Line was occasionally used for special trains and when there were engineering works between Surbiton and Woking. In October 1964, 'West Country' class No. 34093 *Saunton* and Bulleid set No. 770 leaves the New Line just north of Guildford Station.

Plate 70: There was plenty of steam activity at Guildford, despite the predominance of electric trains. It was commonplace to see main line SR built electric units alongside a 2-coach push-pull set hauled or propelled by an ex LSWR Class M7 tank engine. The electric units outlived the old branch stock and motive power, which was replaced by post war vehicles early in the 1960s. In this view of Guildford on 19th October 1963, 2-6-2T Class 2MT No. 41301 leaves for Horsham with SR 3-coach set No. 772. In the background is an 'up' all stations train from Portsmouth & Southsea, consisting of 2-BIL electric units.

GUILDFORD TO BAYNARDS

Plate 71: The old order still survived in 1960 and a train from Cranleigh, on the Horsham branch, is seen at the end of its short journey at Guildford. In this instance the engine is Class 700 No. 30697, hauling two SECR built coaches. Most trains ran the entire length of the branch to Horsham, although there were a few workings which terminated at intermediate stations.

Plate 72: The view from the end of the 'down' platform at Guildford through an arch of the roadbridge, showing the LSWR signal box and engine shed. The train is the 9.08 am to Baynards, worked by Class 2MT No. 41301 on 15th May 1964.

Plate 73: The Horsham branch left the Portsmouth main line at Peasmarsh Junction, two miles south of Guildford and then closely followed the Wey & Arun Junction Canal almost to Cranleigh. Class M7 No. 30109 is photographed on the branch, approaching Peasmarsh Junction with the 9.30 am train from Horsham on 4th May 1958.

Plate 74: Another train near Peasmarsh was photographed almost exactly seven years later. The branch engine is Class 2MT No. 41301 and the coaches of BR origin. The line was closed within six weeks of this visit, the last train being worked by sister engine No. 41287. The site of the junction at Peasmarsh is still visible, although the signal box and railway houses have been demolished. A short length of the trackbed just beyond the junction has been obscured by road improvements, although the course of the railway can be traced for most of its length.

Plate 75: Earlier the same day a Horsham bound train pulls away from Bramley & Wonersh Station. The populations of Bramley and Cranleigh had grown in size as a result of people seeking cheaper housing away from more popular areas such as Surbiton and Woking, and the railway was in a good position to capture additional traffic. From the commuter's point of view, the branch with its access to main line trains to London offered a much better mode of transport to Guildford than the bus, a slow journey fraught with traffic holdups. The morning and evening branch trains were crowded, but the service was sparse and eventually most people found it more convenient to drive to Guildford to catch the London trains. The railways never took advantage of the situation and passenger traffic slowly declined, making closure inevitable.

Plate 76: The line passed through pleasant, but not spectacular countryside, the most interesting parts of the line being the areas around the stations. The 10.34 am Guildford to Horsham train near Cranleigh on 2nd April 1960, propelled by Class M7 No. 30049. The coach next to the engine is an SR 10-compartment all-third vehicle, several examples of which are in use on privately owned lines.

Plate 77: The Guildford to Cranleigh only service passing Cranleigh Yard on 2nd April 1960. Although set No. 663 is fitted for push-pull working, power was provided by an ex LSWR 0-6-0 goods engine, Class 700 No. 30697, which of course was not able to operate in the push-pull mode.

Plate 78: Cranleigh was a well kept station, enhanced in this picture by the presence of the Guildford train, handled by Class H No. 31530. There were both 'up' and 'down' platforms at Cranleigh, but the branch was single track, with passing loops at all stations except Rudgwick and Slinfold. The schedule could be described as leisurely as most trains took about 50 minutes to cover the 20 miles between Guildford and Horsham. Several trains had unnecessarily long scheduled stops at Baynards or Cranleigh, such as this train, the 12.09 pm from Horsham, which had a 13 minute wait here.

Plate 80: The same train four years earlier, with ex LBSCR Class E4 No. 32475 and set No. 600 entering Baynards Station, which was in the most attractive setting on the line. The goods yard can be seen behind the starter on the left of the photograph.

Plate 81: There was a daily freight train from Guildford, which called at intermediate stations as required. On 24th March 1961, Class M7 No. 30132 passes through Baynards on its way to Horsham. Freight consisted mostly of agricultural produce, bricks, timber, coal and chemicals, but gradually this was all lost to road competition and all the goods yards were closed by 1963.

Plate 82: In more prosperous days the goods trains were longer and would usually be required to call at all stations. Class C2X No. 32522 of Horsham shed shunts at Baynards on the morning of 4th March 1958. The longest sidings on the line, which served an earth works, were situated at Baynards.

Plate 83: The 12.21 pm Horsham to Guildford train with Class M7 No. 30049 enters the short tunnel which marks the county boundary with Sussex, just south of Baynards Station on 4th March 1958.

Plate 84: The SR had several different ways of disposing of old or surplus rolling stock. Coaches, if they were not condemned and thence destroyed, were either transferred to the engineer's department and would be used, for example, for mess vans in breakdown trains, or they would be converted for use as static offices or stores. Many pre-Grouping coaches survived in these forms, but even these were eventually scrapped and their place taken by spare Maunsell stock resulting from the Southern Region electrification programme. The most effective way of immobilizing a coach was, of course, to remove the bogies and ground the body. An equally effective means was used at Staines Central in 1966, where an old corridor coach, No. 081152 is seen isolated on its own length of track with buffer stops at both ends! It was built in 1931 as parlour coach No. 7784 and withdrawn from revenue earning service in 1959.

Plate 85: An SR gantry signal at the London end of Staines Central Station. This controls entry to the yard and carriage sidings, as well as including the 'up' starter. It was a misreading of this signal on 9th August 1957 which resulted in a London bound electric train colliding with an engine leaving the yard.

Plate 86: The force of the impact threw the engine, an LSWR Class 700 No. 30688, on its side and caused considerable damage. The front cab of the electric unit was smashed, but fortunately it was a **BR** all steel vehicle and there was little damage to the compartments. It was only a few years prior to this that the service was worked by wooden bodied 2-NOL units. These were withdrawn fairly rapidly, following a disaster in which one caught fire after a serious crash at Barnes. The damaged 700 is seen at Staines Yard the day after the accident. It was later towed to Eastleigh and was broken up the next month.

Plate 87: The 'Remembrance' class consisted of seven engines, rebuilt as 4-6-0s in 1934 from ex LBSCR 4-6-4 tank engines. They were allocated to the Western Section and used on Bournemouth expresses. In later years they were relegated to excursion and relief trains. They ended their days on semi-fast trains and were allocated to Basingstoke for this purpose. No. 32331 *Beattie,* the last survivor, was used on a Ramblers' excursion from London Bridge to Windsor & Eton on 23rd June 1957. Ramblers' excursions were well patronised by railway enthusiasts, as interesting motive power was often used and the routes taken were sometimes unusual. On this occasion the excursion ran via Peckham Rye and Streatham to Wimbledon, where it joined the main line to Weybridge and thence Virginia Water to approach Staines from the country, rather than the London direction. It then traversed the Staines West Curve and thus reached Windsor without the necessity to reverse at Staines Central Station. The return fare for this journey was six shillings. The west curve was later removed, but the direct Waterloo to Windsor line still has a frequent service of electric trains.

STAINES TO ASCOT

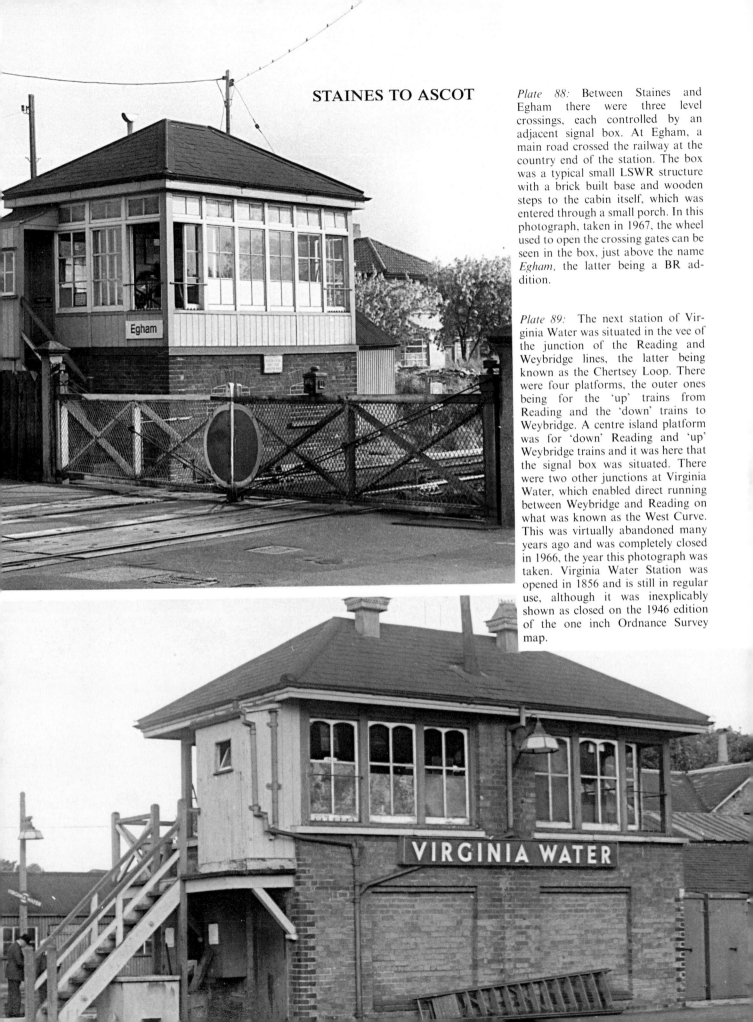

Plate 88: Between Staines and Egham there were three level crossings, each controlled by an adjacent signal box. At Egham, a main road crossed the railway at the country end of the station. The box was a typical small LSWR structure with a brick built base and wooden steps to the cabin itself, which was entered through a small porch. In this photograph, taken in 1967, the wheel used to open the crossing gates can be seen in the box, just above the name *Egham*, the latter being a BR addition.

Plate 89: The next station of Virginia Water was situated in the vee of the junction of the Reading and Weybridge lines, the latter being known as the Chertsey Loop. There were four platforms, the outer ones being for the 'up' trains from Reading and the 'down' trains to Weybridge. A centre island platform was for 'down' Reading and 'up' Weybridge trains and it was here that the signal box was situated. There were two other junctions at Virginia Water, which enabled direct running between Weybridge and Reading on what was known as the West Curve. This was virtually abandoned many years ago and was completely closed in 1966, the year this photograph was taken. Virginia Water Station was opened in 1856 and is still in regular use, although it was inexplicably shown as closed on the 1946 edition of the one inch Ordnance Survey map.

Plate 90: In addition to the passenger services, there were frequent freight trains for both Reading and the main line, the latter being reached by a flyunder at Byfleet Junction. On 14th March 1965, Class 5MT No. 73171 heads for Woking between Egham and Virginia Water. The colour light signals for the junction are visible in the background.

Plate 91: Steam hauled passenger trains were very unusual on this line, but in April 1965 a special is seen approaching Virginia Water behind Class S15 No. 30837. The siding in the foreground ran beside a sanatorium and was occasionally used to dump crippled wagons or failed locomotives.

Plate 92:   Apart from through freight trains on the Chertsey Loop, there was a daily pickup freight which terminated at Weybridge. This was frequently worked by a Class S15 locomotive, such as No. 30833, which was built by the SR in 1927 and is entering Addlestone on 24th July 1963.

Plate 93:   Occasionally the pickup freight would be worked by locomotives of other classes such as SR Q1s and Moguls. On 16th June 1963, Class N No. 31816 was used and is passing the Addlestone distant signal with a few wagons. This was a Feltham duty, although this particular engine is from Eastleigh shed.

Plate 94: This train was a favourite with the author for the simple reason that he saw it most days of the week on his way to work. This was no coincidence, as departure from home at Woking was carefully timed to ensure that this would be so. On occasions when he missed it, it was usually due to late running on the part of the railway, rather than his own form of transport which was the bicycle. This habit had been adopted from regular encounters with the Hampton Court freight train when he lived at Surbiton. On 15th May 1963 the Weybridge freight train is hauled by one of the LSWR built S15s, No. 30512.

Plate 95: Between Virginia Water and Ascot the railway crossed the county boundary separating Surrey and Berkshire. Ascot was the junction for a line through Camberley, which joined the Brookwood to Alton line at Ash Vale (see Plate 47). Waterloo to Reading trains had a portion for this line, which was detached at Ascot and ran to Aldershot. After reversing, it ran on to Guildford, making a total journey time from Waterloo to Guildford of 1³/4 hours, compared with 36 minutes by the fast trains on the direct route through Woking. An interesting contrast with Virginia Water was the signal box at Ascot, which was built by the SR. There were signal boxes of similar design at, for example, Woking and Templecombe, all of which were built shortly before World War II. By Ascot box on 19th May 1962 is Class N No. 31858 and a brake van.

Plate 96: From one extreme to the other. A long freight train by SR standards, hauled by Class S15 No. 30840, approaches Ascot en route to Reading later the same morning.

Plate 97: A rural setting and yet only about 30 miles from London, with the local freight train waiting to leave Camberley in fading light on a November afternoon in 1961. This was an interesting working as Guildford shed usually provided an ex LSWR engine, on this occasion Class 700 No. 30698.

ASCOT TO ASH VALE

Plate 98: The line from Ascot to Ash Vale ran over Bagshot Heath and thence followed the Blackwater River. It was an unexciting line, the only major engineering works being a very high viaduct just south of Bagshot Station. Most of the lines in this part of Surrey were still controlled by semaphore signals in the 1960s and the original LSWR signal boxes were still in use. This photograph shows Camberley box which also controlled the adjacent level crossing. Many level crossing gates were operated manually, but at busy locations such as this, they were mechanically operated.

Plate 99: On the former LBSCR line from London to Horsham and the South Coast (the Mid Sussex Line), the section between Epsom and Leatherhead was jointly operated with the LSWR, although at both these towns each railway had its own station. The LBSCR station at Epsom was situated just before to the intersection of the two lines and was opened in 1847. The LSWR did not reach Epsom until 12 years later and at the same time the joint line to Leatherhead was opened. The LSWR station at Epsom was on the joint line and although the LBSCR station (known as Epsom Town) was superfluous, it did not close until 1929. The same year, the SR opened a new station on the site of the LSWR station. There was a small engine shed adjacent to the Town Station and this too closed in 1929, when electric train services began. The Town Station was then used for all freight traffic for Epsom and it continued in this role for many years. Class U1 No. 31904 shunts at the Town Yard on 28th May 1962.

THE MID SUSSEX LINE

Plate 100: There was an hourly electric train service on the Mid Sussex Line and steam was used only on special passenger trains. On 10th May 1959 a Ramblers' excursion bound for Slinfold on the Horsham to Guildford line is seen near Ewell East, hauled by Class Q No. 30537. Ewell also had a station on the LSWR line, later named Ewell West. The two stations were about a mile apart and being in an area of rapid population expansion, both have survived to enjoy electric train services from Victoria and Waterloo respectively.

Plate 101: A remarkable survivor of the steam era was the Oxted line, which traversed the eastern boundary of Surrey. There were regular steam hauled passenger trains from London to Oxted and thence via East Grinstead to Tunbridge Wells, right up to the modernization of the line in 1965. The northern part of the line had, of necessity, to pass through suburban London and the sight of a steam train amongst the proliferation of electric trains always caused one to look twice. Beyond Croydon, where the line passed into Surrey, the scenery abruptly changed and open country was soon reached. Class 4MT No. 80017 is seen near Sanderstead with the 11.08 am Victoria to Tunbridge Wells West train on 5th September 1959. This train has just passed the corresponding 'up' service, seen in the background.

Plate 102: Emerging from Riddlesdown Tunnel is another engine of the same class, No. 80032 on a train bound for Tunbridge Wells in the Autumn of 1959. Riddlesdown Tunnel, which was cut through chalk typical of the North Downs, was 800 yards long. There was also a station by the name of Riddlesdown, north of the tunnel, which was built 43 years after the opening of the line.

Plate 103: Class U1 No. 31905 on the 12.47 pm London Bridge to Tunbridge Wells West train passing the closed signal box near the tunnel mouth. Shortly after the tunnel, the line crossed a viaduct, where there was a cement works, although there was no rail access. The line climbs all the way from its junction near South Croydon, through Riddlesdown to the summit just beyond Woldingham.

Plate 104:   Pulling away from Upper Warlingham Station on 5th September 1959 is Class U1 No. 31909 on the 2.08 pm Victoria to Tunbridge Wells West train. On the left are the coal sidings, which were closed in 1968. Up to this point the line ran parallel with the Caterham branch, which left the main line at Purley, two miles beyond South Croydon. The Caterham line was built in the valley, whereas the Oxted line climbed to a much higher elevation along the valley side. The two lines were separated by the main A22 road and across this road from Upper Warlingham Station was Whyteleafe on the Caterham line.

Plate 105:   Another train bound for Tunbridge Wells near Woldingham, on this occasion worked by Class 4MT 2-6-4T No. 42067. There were a number of these engines on the Central and Eastern Sections of the Southern Region, which were built at Brighton Works after Nationalization, to an LMSR design. They replaced the pre-Grouping engines previously used and in turn they were superseded by BR Standard tank engines, which were also built at Brighton. A year after this photograph was taken, these engines were transferred to the London Midland and Scottish Regions, No. 42067 being allocated to Bletchley and later to Carlisle.

Plate 106:   There was a regular pattern of services for most of the day, with additional workings in the busy morning and evening periods. At Oxted on 19th May 1961 is Class 4MT No. 75070 on the 5.37 pm London Bridge to East Grinstead train, consisting of a miscellaneous collection of early SR corridor and non-corridor rolling stock. Until the winter of 1953, this train ran beyond East Grinstead to Lewes and Brighton and was often worked by an LBSCR Atlantic locomotive. The East Grinstead to Lewes section was closed in 1958, but part now forms the Bluebell Railway. The engine on the right, Class 4MT No. 80143, is waiting to work a train to Tunbridge Wells West.

Plate 107:   Old and new forms of motive power pass at Oxted. The 'up' train, hauled by Class N No. 31865, is the 8.20 am from Brighton and was one of the several per day which ran via Eridge to Victoria. The diesel multiple unit, No. 1308, is working the 9.09 am Victoria to Tunbridge Wells West train on 16th August 1962. The diesel units for the Oxted services were introduced two months previously and were similar to those built for Hampshire in 1957. The Oxted vehicles were narrower and the main visible differences were that the ends of each unit were rounded and less austere. Nineteen units were built at Eastleigh and they were still in use in 1987.

Plate 108: For most of the day the direct service between Oxted and Tunbridge Wells West was push-pull operated. Class H No. 31193 is shunting set No. 660 at Oxted, prior to forming the 12.04 pm to Tunbridge Wells West on 14th April 1962. Oxted was only 26 miles from London and the presence of push-pull trains added a distinctly rural flavour to the scene.

Plate 109: Evening at Oxted on 14th August 1956, with push-pull trains for the Tunbridge Wells West service. In the bay is Class H No. 31278 and on the 'down' line is No. 31327.

Plate 110: An 'up' empty carriage working to Victoria entering Oxted on 26th May 1962 and hauled by Class 5MT No. 75075. All 'up' and 'down' passenger trains stopped at Oxted, although some did not stop at all intermediate stations and four trains per day ran fast from East Croydon. One evening train split at Oxted, the front portion being for Brighton and the rear for Tunbridge Wells West.

Plate 111: Between Oxted and Hurst Green the line crossed the A25 East to West main road on a high viaduct and a little further on entered a deep cutting, culminating in a tunnel. Leaving the tunnel on 14th April 1960 is the 11.47 am Tunbridge Wells West to Victoria train with Class 4MT No. 80016 at the head.

Plate 112: Seen from the tunnel portal and with the viaduct in the background is a 'down' train on 14th April 1960. A fixed interval service was introduced in 1955 and trains left Victoria for Tunbridge Wells at eight minutes past each hour, this train being the 12.08 pm which is hauled by Class 4MT No. 80154. Motive power for the Oxted line was provided by several sheds. The fitted Class H tanks and several of the BR Standard tank engines were from Tunbridge Wells West shed, whilst the tender engines for the London to Brighton through trains came from Stewarts Lane, Brighton and Three Bridges sheds.

Plate 113: Class H No. 31544 emerging from the other end of the tunnel on the 2.04 pm Oxted to Tunbridge Wells West direct service on 14th April 1960. Two trains, later in the afternoon, continued beyond Tunbridge Wells to Tonbridge on the ex SER main line from London to Dover.

Plate 114: The same engine on one of the most extraordinary passenger train workings on BR, which involved a journey of just one mile. This was the 1.52 pm Hurst Green Halt to Oxted service, which ran on Mondays to Fridays only and which had no balancing 'down' working. It is seen beginning its journey on 14th April 1960, a year prior to closure of the halt, which had been in existence since 1907.

Plate 115: Another unusual feature of Hurst Green was that although it lost its halt, a new station was opened in June 1961, just a few yards to the north. A push-pull train consisting of set No. 655 heading for Oxted and propelled by Class H No. 31544 passes the site of the new station a few months prior to opening.

Plate 116: Between Oxted and East Grinstead was Lingfield, where there was a racecourse and special trains were run in connection with the meetings. On 26th May 1962 three specials were run and one of these, hauled by Class N No. 31828, is passing through Hurst Green Station. Hop pickers' trains from London to the Kent fields also took this route on occasions, reaching Tonbridge via the Crowhurst spur between Hurst Green and Lingfield.

Plate 117: Class H No. 31522 on the 1.04 pm Oxted to Tunbridge Wells West train near Hurst Green on 26th May 1962.

Plate 118: BR Standard Class 4MT No. 80147 with the 1.08 pm Victoria to Tunbridge Wells West train approaching milepost 21¼ near Hurst Green on 14th April 1960. These engines have proved very suitable for present day privately run lines as they are only about 30 years old, quite powerful and yet pose no great weight restrictions. There are at least ten still in existence, some of which are in full working order, including one on the Bluebell Railway only 19 miles south of Hurst Green.

Plate 119: Just south of Hurst Green was the junction of the East Grinstead and the direct Tunbridge Wells lines. On 14th April 1960 the 1.47 pm Tunbridge Wells West to London train was worked by Class 4MT No. 75069 and is seen approaching Hurst Green Junction. A signal on the direct line is just in sight on the left. The signal in the foreground, guarding the junction, is a relic of the LBSCR, with wooden post and arm. It was not taken out of use until 1971 and was probably the last pre-Grouping survivor on the Central Section. The notice cautioning the public before crossing the railway is of SR origin. Cast iron notices of the SECR and LSWR were commonplace at this time, but LBSCR notices were a rarity even in the days immediately succeeding Nationalization.

Plate 124: Outside Redhill shed in May 1962 is 'Schools' class No. 30930 *Radley*. Four 'Schools' class were allocated to Redhill, although the majority of engines allocated here were SR Moguls, there being as many as 18 in 1962.

Plate 125: (Right, top) Reigate was the first station on the line towards Guildford and Reading and was two miles west of Redhill. This short section was electrified in 1932 and was covered by a shuttle service, usually consisting of a 2-BIL unit. This was very frequent in rush hours and during the rest of the day there were two trains per hour in each direction. The steam trains to and from Guildford ran approximately every hour, making Reigate a busy station. The station was at the bottom of Reigate Hill on the main London to Brighton road, which crossed the railway on the level. The frequency of the trains caused considerable delays to road traffic, particularly during the summer when the normal load was augmented by holidaymakers, who would have found it quicker to have used the railway. On 26th May 1962 the 8.20 am train from Reading was worked rather unusually by Class S15 No. 30847, one of four of the class allocated to Redhill. The level crossing is in the background.

Plate 126: (Right) One month previously, the same engine is engaged on duties more in keeping with its role and is on a ballast train at Betchworth. The minor road crossing the railway in the foreground led to a hill known as Pebblecombe, which at its steepest had a gradient of 1 in 6. The author has descended this hill on many occasions dangerously close to the speed limit (on a bicycle!), only to find the crossing gates closed ...

Plate 127: Dorking was the only town of any size between Reigate and Guildford. Indeed there were two stations for Dorking on this line, known as Deepdene and Dorking Town and another station, Dorking North, on the Mid Sussex line. At Dorking Town on a wet afternoon in May 1962 is Class U1 No. 31890 and set No. 187 on the 2.50 pm Reading to Redhill service. The platforms at this station are staggered in typical SECR style, the only other station on this line with the same layout being Gomshall & Shere.

Plate 128: On 15th May 1964, with the arrival of diesels only months away, Class N No. 31412 approaches the summit of the climb from Dorking on the 1.35 pm train from Redhill with set No. 444. Despite running east to west parallel with the Surrey Hills, the line was surprisingly heavily graded.

Plate 129: 'Schools' class No. 30911 *Dover* with a train of BR built coaches forming the 9.15 am Margate to Wolverhampton train, passing through Gomshall & Shere Station on 28th April 1962. This was the only train of the day to run non stop between Redhill and Guildford. Beyond Guildford it stopped only at North Camp before reaching the Western Region at Reading General. The train did not run in the heart of winter, but started early in May and ran daily until the end of October. The journey time from Redhill to Reading was 1 hour 17 minutes, only 12 minutes slower than the present day diesel multiple unit trains calling at the same stations.

Plate 130: Despite the legend on the leading vehicle, this train is actually at Gomshall & Shere and the author has no idea why the car carrier was so far from home territory. The remaining vehicles of this train were passenger coaches and formed the 11.05 am Reading to Redhill service with Class N No. 31869 on 28th April 1962.

Plate 131: Class S15 No. 30835 near Gomshall & Shere working a freight train to Reading in April 1962.

Plate 132: Another Reading to Redhill train with a 'foreign' van, this time an LNER full brake, which together with a BR three-coach set forms the 12.05 pm train. It is hauled by Class U No. 31636 and is entering Chilworth & Albury Station. It was surprising to find a country station with a footbridge linking the platforms. Dorking Town had a subway and at Deepdene the only way to cross from the 'up' to the 'down' platform was to leave the station altogether and pass under the road bridge by the station. At Gomshall & Shere a boarded crossing only was provided.

Plate 133: From 4th January 1965 the line was, at least officially, worked by diesel multiple units, although in practice steam working persisted. Later the same month, Class N No. 31862 works a Redhill to Reading train and is seen near Albury.

Plate 134: On 4th May 1963, Class N No. 31852 is photographed near Shalford on the 8.20 am train from Reading, the leading set being No. 466.

Plate 135: Entering Shalford on 15th May 1964 is the 9.45 am Reading to Redhill train hauled by Class U No. 31639. Shalford was only two miles from Guildford and the railway suffered from road competition as it ran parallel with roads from both Godalming and Horsham (see Plate 75). Shalford and all the other stations between Redhill and Reading are still open, although some of the intermediate stations have a very poor service.

Plate 136: Former GWR locomotives were fairly common on this line in the summer months, as they were permitted to work right through on inter regional trains. On 27th August 1960, Class 4300 No. 5332 of Carmarthen shed works the 10.45 am from Birmingham and is crossing the River Wey between Guildford and Shalford, near the junction with the LSWR main line to Portsmouth. The train conveyed through coaches for Brighton and Hastings and ran only on summer Saturdays. The engine was taken off at Redhill and prepared for its return journey, when it worked the 4.04 pm local train to Reading South.

Plate 137: Most trains ran the whole length of the line, but a few ran only as far as Guildford from both the Reading and Redhill directions. One such train was the 9.43 am from Redhill which, on 27th August 1960 was worked by Class U No. 31627 and set No. 190. It is seen at Guildford, ready for berthing.

Plate 138: Immediately outside Guildford the Reading line turned west, away from the Waterloo to Portsmouth line and climbed round the northern edge of Stag Hill. It then passed over Broadstreet Common, which was an excellent place to view the trains, although it was not accessible by road and in the winter was windswept and wet under foot. A Reading to Redhill train passes a 2-BIL electric unit heading for Aldershot on the common on the last day of 1964.

Plate 139: Another 2-BIL unit, on this occasion No 2151 at Ash Junction on 30th May 1963. The direct line to Farnham through Tongham is in the foreground, which was closed to passengers in 1937 but the freight service was retained as far as Tongham. The Tongham line was single throughout and never electrified. Farnham can still be reached from Guildford by changing at Aldershot.

Plate 140: Class U No. 31625 on the 3.04 pm Redhill to Reading train passing the disused signal gantry at Ash Junction. The leading vehicle is one of the impressive SR built bogie brake and luggage vans.

Plate 141: Sandhurst was on the boundary of three counties, Hampshire, Surrey and Berkshire, the halt itself being in Berkshire. Sandhurst Halt was opened three years after completion of the line, but closed a year later in 1853. It was reopened in 1909 and is still open at the time of writing, it now being called simply Sandhurst. Approaching the halt on 25th May 1963 is BR Standard Class 4MT No. 75070 with the 11.05 am train from Reading. Semaphore signals were used on most of the line, but this section was controlled by colour light signals as seen in the background.

Plate 142: Former GWR 'Manor' Class No 7813 *Freshford Manor* of Tyseley shed brings two 2-coach Maunsell sets into Crowthorne on the 12.37 pm Guildford to Reading train on 25th May 1963. The original station buildings on the Guildford side still exist. They are in an appalling state and all doors and windows have been bricked up following extensive vandalism. A small modern shelter is all that is provided on the other side.

Plate 143: A freight train from Reading hauled by Class Q1 No. 33019 passes through Crowthorne in May 1963.

Plate 144: Standard Class 4MT No. 80137 on the 12.18 pm train from Reading leaving Crowthorne in May 1963. This engine was formerly of Tunbridge Wells West shed, but along with several sister engines had recently been transferred to work the Reading to Redhill services following dieselization of the Oxted line (see Plate 106).

Plate 145: The size of the SR facilities at Reading can be judged from this plate, taken from the window of a train on the Western Region main line on 25th March 1956. The locomotive shed is on the right hand side and the goods yard in the background. The running roads into Reading South Station pass in front of the signal box and the lines in the foreground connect the Southern and Western Regions. The station was renamed Reading Southern in 1960, but despite its obviously busy nature, it was completely closed in 1965 and all facilities transferred to Reading General. Reading General thus became even more congested, particularly following the introduction of additional trains to Guildford and Gatwick Airport. It is interesting that, at the time of writing, a new station is under construction using in part the very area once occupied by the SR.

Tailpiece: The approach to Weybridge is through a deep cutting with concrete retaining walls. A road passes over the London end of the station and coming under the bridge in August 1961 is 'Merchant Navy' class, No. 35017, *Belgian Marine* on a 'down' extra Bournemouth train.

Appendix I – Index of Motive Power

Appendix II – Index of Passenger Rolling Stock